MATH IT!

WEIGH IT!

by Nadia Higgins

pogo

Ideas for Parents and Teachers

Pogo Books let children practice reading informational text while introducing them to nonfiction features such as headings, labels, sidebars, maps, and diagrams, as well as a table of contents, glossary, and index.

Carefully leveled text with a strong photo match offers early fluent readers the support they need to succeed.

Before Reading

- "Walk" through the book and point out the various nonfiction features. Ask the student what purpose each feature serves.
- Look at the glossary together. Read and discuss the words.

Read the Book

- Have the child read the book independently.
- Invite him or her to list questions that arise from reading.

After Reading

- Discuss the child's questions. Talk about how he or she might find answers to those questions.
- Prompt the child to think more. Ask: Look around you. What do you see that you could weigh? Of these things, what do you think is the heaviest? How about the lightest?

Pogo Books are published by Jump!
5357 Penn Avenue South
Minneapolis, MN 55419
www.jumplibrary.com

Copyright © 2017 Jump!
International copyright reserved in all countries.
No part of this book may be reproduced in any form without written permission from the publisher.

Library of Congress Cataloging-in-Publication Data

Names: Higgins, Nadia, author.
Title: Weigh it! / by Nadia Higgins.
Description: Minneapolis, MN: Jump!, Inc. [2016] | © 2017
Series: Math it!
Audience: Ages 7-10.
Includes bibliographical references and index.
Identifiers: LCCN 2016011648 (print)
LCCN 2016014400 (ebook)
ISBN 9781620314111 (hardcover: alk. paper)
ISBN 9781624964589 (ebook)
Subjects: LCSH: Weight (Physics)—Measurement—Juvenile literature.
Measurement—Juvenile literature.
Classification: LCC QC106 .H54 2016 (print)
LCC QC106 (ebook) | DDC 530.8—dc23
LC record available at http://lccn.loc.gov/2016011648

Series Editor: Jenny Fretland VanVoorst
Series Designer: Anna Peterson
Photo Researcher: Anna Peterson

Photo Credits: All photos by Shutterstock except: Adobe Stock, 23; Dreamstime, 17; Getty, 8-9, 10, 11; iStock, 4, 5; Thinkstock, 4, 6-7, 12-13.

Printed in the United States of America at Corporate Graphics in North Mankato, Minnesota.

TABLE OF CONTENTS

CHAPTER 1

· ·

A-WEIGH WE GO!

A wand of cotton candy. A fresh green apple. Which of these is heavier?

Put one in each hand. Hold out your arms. Even though it is smaller, the apple feels heavier.

Let's check with a scale. The cotton candy weighs 2 ounces. The apple weighs 4 ounces. The apple *is* heavier.
Now you know for sure.

Cotton Candy = 2 Ounces
Apple = 4 Ounces

Weight is a measurement that shows how heavy things are.

Why is weight important? Imagine you are going on a trip. The airline charges extra for bags over 50 pounds.

Will Dad have to pay extra for his suitcase? Weight it!

The scale says it is a pound over. He'll need to take something out.

Frankie the dog is too squirmy to stand on a scale. Try this trick to weigh him.

First, you step on the scale. Record your weight.

Next, hold Frankie and step on the scale. How much do you and Frankie weigh together?

Do subtraction to find Frankie's weight.

MY WEIGHT: 86 POUNDS

COMBINED WEIGHT: 118 POUNDS

118 − 86 = 32

FRANKIE'S WEIGHT: 32 POUNDS

CHAPTER 2

· ·

KNOW YOUR UNITS

Alfie the rabbit weighs 18 ounces. We could also say that Alfie is 1 pound, 2 ounces. Why?

Because 1 pound has 16 ounces. Do the math: 16 ounces + 2 ounces = 18 ounces, Alfie's weight.

Let's weigh Alfie using the **metric system**. Most people in the world use this system of measurement.

The metric system makes it easy to switch from one **unit** to another. All units are in **multiples** of 10. For example, a kilogram equals 1,000 grams.

Alfie weighs 510 grams. That is about half of 1,000. So Alfie weighs about half a kilogram.

Tons are used to measure very heavy things. A ton is 2,000 pounds, or 907 kilograms. A metric ton is heavier. It's 1,000 kilograms, or 2,204 pounds.

The giraffe on the left weighs about 1 ton.

The giraffe on the right weighs 1 metric ton. That makes him a little heavier. How much heavier? He's 204 pounds heavier.

DID YOU KNOW?

By law, trucks are not allowed to weigh too much. They need to stop at **weigh stations** along the highway. A truck drives right onto a giant scale that measures in tons.

1,000 Kilograms =
1 Metric Ton

2,000 Pounds =
1 Ton

CHAPTER 3

....

WEIGH SMART

Let's visit a farm and weigh some things there. What units make the most sense for each item? Choose ounces, pounds, or tons.

Now let's measure in metric. What things would you weigh using grams?

How about kilograms or metric tons?

Let's weigh the piglet on a **dial scale**. The needle starts at 0. It moves around the circle, like the hands on a clock. The more the needle moves, the more the piglet weighs.

This scale measures in pounds. The needle is pointing at 5.

The piglet weighs 5 pounds.

THINK ABOUT IT!

What if the needle were halfway between 5 and 6? How much would the piglet weigh?

2,268g

Now weigh the piglet on a **digital scale**. Just read the number on the display. Wait a minute—the piglet weighs 2,268?

Whoops! The display says *g* for grams. Press the button to switch to *lb.* for pounds. The unit makes a big difference!

Now you know your units. So choose the best one. Read your scale carefully. Go ahead—weigh it!

ACTIVITIES & TOOLS

TRY THIS!

MAKE YOUR OWN BALANCE

Make your own balance to compare the weight of two objects around the house.

What You Need:
- two paper plates
- a hole punch
- string
- scissors
- a hanger with notches at either end

❶ Punch four holes evenly spaced around the edge of each plate.

❷ Cut eight pieces of string about 2 feet (60 centimeters) long.

❸ Divide the string into two groups of four. Tie each together at one end.

❹ Take one bunch of string and thread each strand through a hole in the plate. Turn the plate over and tie a knot at the end of each string. Do the same with the second plate and bunch of string.

❺ Hang each plate from one end of the hanger. Use the hanger's notches so the strings will not slip. Arrange two strings to hang in the front of the hanger and two strings to hang in the back.

❻ Find a place to hang your balance where the plates can dangle freely. Then find objects to compare. Put one item on each plate. How do you know which is heavier? The heavier side dips lower than the lighter one.

GLOSSARY

dial scale: A scale that uses a needle that points to numbers to show weight.

digital scale: An electronic scale that shows weight as numbers in a display.

metric system: A system of measurement used by most of the world. Grams, kilograms, and metric tons are units of the metric system.

multiple: A number that can be made by adding together two or more of another, smaller number. For example, 20 is a multiple of 10.

unit: A fixed amount that is used to weigh things. Ounces and pounds are units.

weigh stations: Places along the highway where trucks pull up to get weighed on giant scales.

INDEX

TO LEARN MORE

Learning more is as easy as 1, 2, 3.

1) Go to www.factsurfer.com

2) Enter "weighit" into the search box.

3) Click the "Surf" button to see a list of websites.

With factsurfer, finding more information is just a click away.